communications

© Aladdin Books Ltd 1994

Designed and produced by
Aladdin Books Ltd
28 Percy Street
London W1P 9FF

First published in
the United States in 1994 by
Twenty-First Century Books
A Division of Henry Holt and Company, Inc.
115 West 18th Street
New York, NY 10011
Hawkes, Nigel

Library of Congress Catologing-in-publication data
      Communications / Nigel Hawkes – 1st ed.
          p. cm. – (New technology)
      Includes index
      ISBN 0–8050–3420–X
      1. Telecommunication – Juvenile literature
(1. Telecommunication. 2. Communication.)
I. Title. II. Series.
TK5102.4.H39   1994
621.382–dc20   94-6676   CIP   AC

Design
David West
Children's Book Design
Designers
Edward Simkins
Flick Killerby
Editor
Susannah Le Besque
Research
Brooks Krikler Research
Illustrators
Alex Pang
Peter Harper

Printed in Belgium

new TECHNOLOGY
communications

NIGEL HAWKES

TWENTY-FIRST CENTURY BOOKS
A Division of Henry Holt and Company/New York

CONTENTS

Photocredits
Abbreviations: t-top, m-middle, b-bottom, l-left, r-right
Cover tr, 6, 7 both: IBM UK Ltd; Cover br & l, 4m, 15b, 19br, 21:
Sony UK; Cover tl, 4b: Psion Plc; Cover ml, 6-7, 10m, 11b, 19bl, 23t:
Roger Vlitos; Cover m, back cover, 4t, 19t: VLSI; 3, 26: National
Westminster Bank Plc; 4-5, 18-19, 29b: JVC; 5mr, 9tr & l, 16m,
24m , 25t: Science Photo Library; 8mr & l, 12m, 22, 27t:
Solution Pictures; 9b: 5bl, 8b: Apple Computer UK Ltd; 8-9, 11t,
14m, 15t & m, 20-21, 30b: Frank Spooner Pictures; 9b: Quantel;
10b, 10-11: The Computability Centre; 12b, 12-13: Heriot -Watt
University, Edinburgh; 13 all: Cable & Wireless Marine; 14t, 14-15,
29m: NASA; 16-17, 17, 25b: Philips Consumer Electronics; 18:
Sharp Electronics UK Ltd; 20 both, 24t, 24-25, 25m: Bang &
Olufsen UK Ltd; 23b: Graphics Technology International/Kodak
Ltd; 27m, 30m: British Telecommunications Picture Library; 28 all:
Hulton Deutsch, 29t University of Pennsylvania; 30t: Charles de Vere.

INTRODUCTION
N E W   T E C H N O L O G Y

Humans need to communicate in order to exchange ideas and understand one another's actions. The twentieth century has been witness to an ongoing technological revolution in personal and mass communications. Today the telephone is commonplace; we are able to watch events in remote parts of the world as they happen, and vast quantities of information are sent across the globe in an instant. This book looks at the latest technological breakthroughs in mass and personal communications, and examines by which means we are likely to communicate in the future.

GLASS FIBER
OPTICAL CABLES

Glass-fiber cables are at the heart of today's communication revolution. Thousands of miles of glass-fiber cables are being installed around the world, creating "data highways" along which a variety of information and services can travel. Glass fiber was first introduced to replace copper telephone cables. Capable of carrying 40,000 calls at the same time, the first long-distance glass-fiber telephone cable went into operation in 1983. Today, glass fiber carries far more than telephone calls. It is used to link up computer systems so that large amounts of data can be sent around the world, and to carry signals for cable TV. Recent developments in technology mean that glass fiber can potentially carry 500 TV channels.

The cables (right) are made of fine fibers of glass. Although glass is usually a brittle, fragile material, the quartz glass used for the fibers is tough, flexible, and cheaper than copper. Many fibers are spun together to form cables. These are clad in a tough plastic sheath to protect them from damage.

The first transatlantic glass-fiber cable was laid in 1988, linking Britain and France with the United States. Special ships (left) are used to lay cables. The cables are payed out slowly over the stern of the ship and come to rest on the seabed.

Glass fibers are used to link together computers so that they can communicate with one another, locally or nationally. Japan plans a glass-fiber system that will link virtually every home and office by 2015.

Cables are brought ashore at each end and are linked into the telephone network. Communications satellites share the market with undersea cables, but have yet to replace them.

Undersea cables have to be armored to protect them from accidental damage. In shallow water they are buried to avoid damage from ships' anchors.

G L A S S   F I B E R
H O W   I T   W O R K S

A caller's voice, picked up by a microphone inside the telephone, is converted into digital signals. These turn a laser on and off, sending light pulses along the glass fiber. Each fiber consists of a core of glass surrounded by an outer layer of glass with a lower refractive index. This reflects light at a slightly different angle and stops the light escaping from the fiber. The receiving phone decodes the digital signal. Computer information is transmitted in the same way.

Outer layer of glass

Light path

Glass core

SATELLITES
SPACE COMMUNICATION

Communications satellites (comsats) are capable of relaying computer data, radio, telephone, and TV signals across the world in seconds.

Today, there are hundreds of comsats in orbit around the earth. Now there are plans to build a satellite network far bigger than any of the present systems. Made up of 840 satellites, the network would provide communications services even to the remotest parts of the world. The network would provide a global information network, linking computers in homes and offices.

Consisting of 18 satellites 11,000 miles above the earth, GPS works out the position of the ship or plane by calculating the time the satellite's signal takes to reach the receiver on earth.

SATELLITES
HOW THEY ARE LAUNCHED

Comsats are launched into orbit by rockets (above) or carried into space by space shuttles. Satellites are equipped with booster engines that guide them into orbit and help to keep them there. Earth stations receive telephone, TV, or radio signals and send them to the satellite. The satellite amplifies the signals and retransmits them to earth using a device called a transponder.

Equipped with portable satellite transmitters, journalists can now use comsats to send live broadcasts home without having to rely on the facilities of local TV stations. Aircraft and shipping use a satellite navigation system called the American Global Positioning System (GPS). Portable receivers, such as the Sony Pyxis, make GPS more widely available.

Equipped with portable satellite transmitters (right), newspaper and TV correspondents no longer have to relay live broadcasts via a local TV station with access to a satellite, neither do they have to rely on telephone links.

The Gulf War of 1991 provided an excellent opportunity to test the portable satellite transmitters in action (below). Reporting a war is difficult as well as dangerous, because normal communications are often disrupted. Portable transmitters could transform the coverage of wars and events in remote places.

The Global Positioning System was originally designed for military purposes, but it can also be used by sailors, climbers, explorers, and scientists. The small Sony receiver, called Pyxis (left) after the Pyxis or Compass constellation has opened up GPS to many more people. GPS allows users to know their position anywhere on earth within 30 ft, their speed to within inches per second, and the time to within fractions of a second. With the aid of GPS, scientists in Cumbria, England, have tracked the movements of individual sheep to see why some are still picking up radioactivity from the 1986 Chernobyl disaster.

Astronauts maneuver a satellite into orbit from the space shuttle (above). Other spacecraft can launch satellites but only the space shuttle can be reused. Space shuttles have made it possible to retrieve satellites so they can be serviced in space. Those that need repairs can be brought back to earth.

SONY

PYXIS

GLOBAL POSITIONING SYSTEM

SONY

POS   NAV   TRACK   EDIT   SET   MARK

EXTENSION

CLEAR   RECALL   ENTER

GLOBAL POSITIONING SYSTEM IPS-360

TELEPHONES
L I V E   W I R E S

Today, telephone technology is used for more than just conversations. The diversification of telephone technology is partly due to the replacement of copper telephone cables with glass-fiber cables. These are capable of carrying vast quantities of television signals and computer data. Computers are linked into the phone network so that data can be sent around the globe directly from one computer to another. Mobile phones allow us to talk to anyone from anywhere. They are not connected to the phone system by wires; instead they use a network of radio transmitters.

The first mobile phones were heavy and clumsy. Today's versions, such as the one below left and the Sony mobile phone (right), are small enough to slip into a pocket. The next generation of mobile phones will not be reliant on the cellular network. Instead the calls will be relayed directly by a comsat.

Fifty years ago, there was little choice in telephone models. Today, hundreds of different models are available. A Swedish company, Bang & Olufsen, has developed special loudspeakers to make voices sound more lifelike.

In the United States and Europe videophones are being produced. These use ordinary phone lines and sockets to send moving images of callers as they speak. Videophones allow people who live apart to "see" each other.

MOBILE PHONES
CELLULAR NETWORKS

Mobile phones are fitted with radio transmitters and receivers. To make connections, countries are divided up into different areas known as "cells." The diagram on the right shows how the UK is divided up. A densely populated area, such as Los Angeles or London, is divided up into many small cells, because there are likely to be more people using mobile phones. Where there are fewer people, the cells are bigger. Each cell has its own transmitter. This passes on the conversations to a central control station, which links with the normal telephone network. When a user moves from one cell to the next, the mobile phone automatically changes frequency so that conversations can continue without a break. Because mobile phones use radio waves, conversations can be illegally picked up by strangers who tune into the same frequency.

Cells

Transmitter

Central control station

In the United States satellite and videophone technology is being used to provide medical expertise to remote areas. The doctor (above) is examining X-rays sent via a satellite. Another system allows specialists to watch on screen while they guide local doctors in the examination of a patient.

CD-I – CD-ROM
DIGITAL SOUND & PICTURES

CD-ROM (Compact Disk Read Only Memory) is capable of storing large amounts of information – such as sound, graphics, moving images, and text. Encyclopedias and computer games have been available on CD-ROM for some time. They are accessed by a computer equipped with special software and a CD-ROM drive. Compact Disk Interactive (CD-I) from Philips, uses CD-ROM technology to store information, which is is accessed by a CD-I player that plugs into a TV.

Scanning movement

Light detector

Rotating disk

laser

The laser points at the underside of the CD as it spins. The pits are read by the laser and checked for errors.

A CD-ROM disk can store 800 megabytes of information – the equivalent of about 300,000 pages of text.

PHILIPS

CD-I

Using menus and a hand controller, CD-I gives you much more scope than CD-ROM to interact with the text, pictures, animation, and sound stored on the disk. CD-I based games are already available. Some rock groups have experimented with CD-I, allowing you to mix your own version of the music and images.

The first interactive movie that allows you to direct the plot is now available on CD-I. More are in production. The quality of movies played from a Philips CD-I machine (below) is far better than videotape. Each disk is capable of storing 74 minutes of video.

The Digital Compact Cassette (DCC) recorder plays cassettes that have been recorded digitally. This gives a far higher quality of sound than an ordinary cassette and is just as portable. The advantage over a CD is that you can use them for home recording.

CD-I – CD-ROM
COMPACT STORAGE

CD-ROM stores information digitally – as a set of binary numbers (zero or one). These are recorded as a series of minute pits that lie in spirals less than one thousandth of an inch apart on the underside of the CD. The pits are read by a laser beam and converted back into sound and images. The flexibility of this system of storage means that it is possible to jump instantly from one piece of information to the next – similar to the way you can jump from track to track on an audio CD.

TELEVISION
VIEWING THE FUTURE

Television as we know it is about to be transformed. Soon it will be possible to receive more than 500 cable TV channels – more than six times the number currently available.

This revolution is being made possible by new high-capacity glass-fiber cable. Another recent development is video on demand (VOD), which is now available in some hotels. There are no videotapes involved. Instead your request is passed via your TV to a computer that stores hundreds of movies. The computer then sends the movie of your choice to your TV through the cable network.

Bang & Olufsen has pioneered integrated audio-visual systems (right). The hi-fi, TV, and VCR are all linked and controlled from one remote control. All sound is played through one set of speakers.

Today's "flat" TVs (above) use more compact components and focusing systems to create a slimmer model. Older TVs were often as deep as they were wide, making it difficult to find space for them. In future it may be possible to make a TV that is flat enough to hang on the wall like a picture, using a liquid crystal screen.

Gogglevox (above) has two miniature liquid crystal display screens – one in front of each eye – and stereo earphones. Because the screens are so close to the eyes, the wearer has a sense of *"wraparound" vision. Small magnifying lenses in the headset allow the eyes to focus. The screens are coated with a substance that optically smooths the image.*

Interactive channels broadcast over short distances are planned. These will allow viewers to control the plots of programs recorded on CD-ROM. Direct satellite broadcasts will add high-definition channels to what will be a vast choice. Wide-screen TVs are being introduced. These are more suited to our natural field of vision.

HIGH-DEFINITION TV
A CLEARER PICTURE

Ordinary TVs produce a picture from 525 horizontal lines of information, no matter how big the screen. High-definition TV produces sharper pictures by increasing the number to 1,000 or more. However, HDTV requires new cameras, TV sets, and VCRs, making it expensive to introduce.

Multi-purpose remote controls send an infrared beam coded for each channel to the TV, VCR, or hi-fi. Sensors in each pick up the code.

Wide-screen TVs, which are a third wider than ordinary TVs, are now available. They are being introduced because the human eye's natural field of vision is one third wider than a normal TV screen.

CAMERAS
FUTURE IN MOTION

Television cameras and home video cameras record images in the same way. The camera lens focuses light from an image on to three detectors – one sensitive to green light, one to blue, and the third to red light. The intensity of the light in each color is converted into electrical signals that can be stored on videotape. The camera scans the image it is recording 25 times every second, and converts the image into 525 lines of information. A new form of video has recently been launched called digital video, which uses compact disk technology to store movies and can be played on a CD-I player. Just like music tracks on an ordinary CD, each movie scene can be individually numbered and called up instantly.

Camcorders have built-in infrared beams that measure the range and focus the camera. Electronic circuits measure light intensity, and a recording head transfers the signal onto videotape.

Microphone

Vidicon tube

Lens group

Most camcorders have a viewfinder through which you have to look with one eye to see the recording image. With the Viewcam (left) you can see the image being recorded on a large screen. This gives you a much better idea of what your finished video will be like.

Small video cameras mounted in buildings or in city centers (right) are used as the "eyes" of the police and security guards. They feed their signals directly to screens, and their output is also recorded on VCR. Trouble can be spotted quickly, and evidence stored on videotape can be used to identify thieves.

Viewfinder

Super VHS
VideoMovie S-VHS-C

HQ
High Quality

Video drum

The world's smallest video camera, the Peach camera, was developed by a team at a Scottish university. Barely one inch square and one inch deep, it consists of a lens feeding directly into a microchip. This generates an electrical charge proportional to the light falling on it. This is passed to a monitor or VCR. It is claimed to be at least 20 times smaller than any other TV camera.

SILICON CHIPS
HOW THEY ARE MADE

Silicon chips are at the heart of camcorders and VCRs. Thin wafers of pure silicon are layered with silicon oxide.
1 A mask – a sheet with the circuit pattern printed on it – is put on top. 2 This is etched with acids to expose the silicon. Chemicals called dopants are added. 3 This process is repeated to create circuits. Silicon is a semiconductor, which means its resistance to an electrical current increases as its temperature rises.

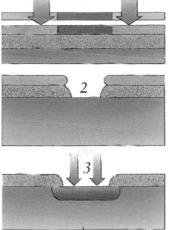

Silicon

The miniaturization of components with the introduction of the silicon chip has made TV cameras increasingly lighter and smaller. Modern TV cameras can easily be carried on the shoulder, or, in the case of the world's smallest camcorder, in one hand (right).

PRINTING
COMPUTERIZED PRINTERS

Today we have a wider choice of books, magazines, and newspapers than ever before. This is due to the introduction of new technology that has transformed printing methods.

Large commercial printing companies are using computer systems that link the printing presses to a computer terminal. From this one person can control all aspects of the printing process, such as how many copies are printed, what size paper is used, and how much ink is required. The computer provides up-to-the minute information on how each print job is progressing. Making a printing plate – which has on it the image from which all copies are printed – is a long and costly process. It normally involves creating images on photographic film, which are then transferred onto the plate. A new process called Direct Imaging bypasses this stage. The image is transferred from a computer directly onto the printing plate.

A laser printer builds up patterns of electrical charges on the surface of a drum. A laser beam bounces off a spinning mirror. This transmits the shapes of the letters, in the form of very fine dots, to the surface of the drum. Powdered ink sticks to the dots on the drum. This is transferred to the paper and made permanent by heating.

Spinning mirror

Laser

Rotating drum

Circuit boards

Rollers

Paper

Toner cartridge

Paintjet or inkjet printers work by firing tiny drops of ink at the paper. The drops, produced at the rate of 100,000 a second, are electrically charged. Electric fields controlled by the computer guide the ink drops to the right spot on the paper. Each letter is formed from about 1,000 drops.

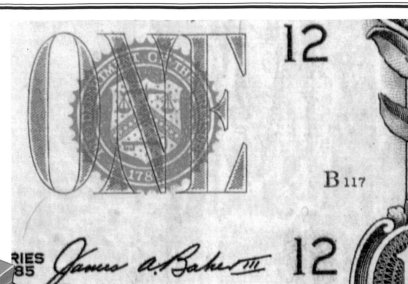

Office laser printers are fast and produce high-quality print. Some laser printers can now print in full color. They are ideal for companies who do not want the expense of using a commercial printer but require a small number of high-quality documents.

Bank notes are printed on special paper and have detailed designs to make counterfeiting difficult. A printing method called photogravure is used, which has long-lasting printing plates and produces the best quality print. Color photocopies of a bank note may look authentic at first glance. A closer look shows that the image is made up of a pattern of dots that is not on the original.

HEAT-SENSITIVE FILM
CHEMICAL-FREE PROCESSING

The Xerox Corporation in Canada has come up with a new type of photographic film that could revolutionize the printing industry. The film, called VerdFilm, can be developed in daylight (left) using heat rather than chemicals. VerdFilm is coated with an element called selenium, which becomes light-sensitive only when it is electrically charged. Once electrically charged, it is heated, causing selenium atoms to fall vertically into the film to reveal the image. VerdFilm does not require a darkroom. It does not require large amounts of energy or water to develop it, nor are there any dangerous waste chemicals.

LANGUAGE
WRITING AND SPEECH

Language and writing as ways of communicating are unique to humans. Computers are now sophisticated enough to be able to read handwriting, to translate speech into written words, and even to help restore the power of speech.

IBM has come up with a computer that is capable of converting speech into the written word. The user speaks into a microphone and the computer analyzes the words that have been spoken. These are displayed on a computer screen at a rate of 70 to 100 per minute. The text can be edited using a keyboard, and then printed out.

For people who have restricted use of their hands, computer keyboards can be customized. The keyboard below is designed to be operated using the end of a pencil. This keyboard has a rigid metal "keyguard" with holes above each key so that users can rest the whole weight of their hands on the keyboard while they locate the key they want to press.

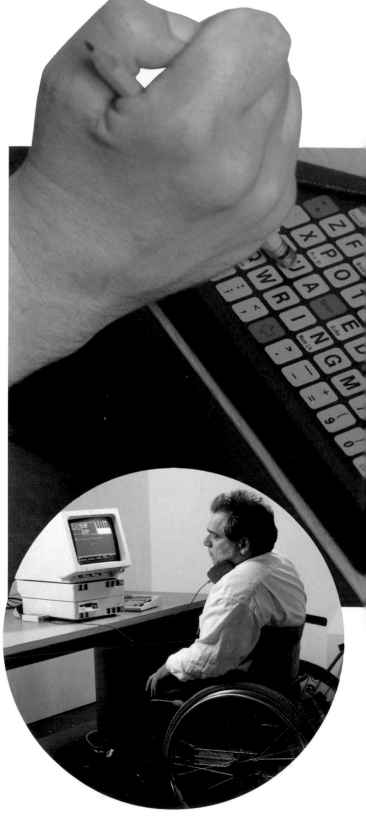

The fax modem (above) converts computer information into electrical signals so they can be sent over the telephone system. The modem connects the computer to this network via an ordinary phone socket.

The development of computer technology has given many disabled people the opportunity to communicate effectively. The man shown on the right is operating his computer with a switch operated by his chin.

THE ELECTRONIC BIBLE
THE POCKET GOSPEL

The Bible has been produced in many forms since it was first handwritten and illuminated by monks. Today, an electronic version of the Bible is being sold by the Franklin Computer Corporation. Weighing only 12.5 ounces, the device stores the entire text of the Bible, in either the Revised Standard or King James version, and displays the text four lines at a time on the screen. The Electronic Bible can be used to locate particular passages of the text. A keyword or phrase is simply typed in, and the phrase or passage is located. The screen scrolls forward so the entire verse or chapter can be read.

With the Newton Notepad the user does not have to tap in information using a keyboard. Instead it is able to recognize handwriting. Using a special pen, all you have to do is write down the information you want to record on its liquid crystal display screen. Or you can draw simple diagrams that it will convert into neat geometric drawings. This is recorded in the Newton Notepad's memory.

The Newton Notepad has a diary and a name file function. The name file lets you record, access, and update the names, addresses, and telephone numbers of friends or relatives. You can also send or receive faxes via the Newton Notepad by connecting it to the phone network using a fax modem.

World-famous British physics professor Stephen Hawking has lost the ability to speak. But a device called a speech synthesizer gives him a voice by saying the words he types on a computer screen.

COMPUTERS
THE NEW INTELLIGENCE

The basis of computer programming is to produce plans that enable problems to be solved by the computer step by step. Every step has to be planned in advance.

A computer can be programmed to play chess, not through intelligence, but by listing the millions of possible moves and choosing the most appropriate. Now scientists are taking a new approach. They are trying to make computers "learn" in much the same way as the human brain, rather than being programmed. A computer called NETalk learned to speak by listening to a child. After 16 hours the computer had a vocabulary of about 1,000 words. But for computers to have human traits such as common sense is a long way off.

WABOT-2

The WABOT robotic hand has 14 joints. Materials that "remember" their original shape are used to operate the joints. This gives the hand dexterity and a gentle touch.

While scientists develop intelligent computers, advances are being made in home computers. The new generation of Apple computers (left and right) are the first commercially available computers to have a speech recognition system with menus that can be operated by voice commands.

NEURAL NETS
NEW COMPUTER LOGIC

"Intelligent" computers are called neural nets, because they try to copy the behavior of human brain cells, or neurons, that form a network in the brain. In a conventional computer, the circuits operate one after another, processing data as it flows through. In the brain, and in neural nets, all circuits work at once. Conventional computers are given programs to guide them. Neural nets learn by repetition and learn from their mistakes.

This robot (left) is used for undersea research. It is capable of performing simple tasks, but it does not do this intelligently.

In the future, computers may be multi-screened like the one below, so it will be possible to work on a number of different projects simultaneously.

Artists use a computer graphics program (below) to design on screen with the aid of a computerized drawing board and pen.

NETWORKS
ELECTRONIC INFORMATION

Computer networks have a wide variety of functions. British Telecom has developed an interactive computer network for designers so that people in different locations can work on the same design.

An American retail company plans to install a computerized catalogue in its shops. Customers will be able to view the range of products at the touch of a button. Smart cards look like credit cards but because they are fitted with a microchip, sums of money can be stored on them. This type of card is currently in use in many cities throughout the United States for mass transit. Each time the user enters the turnstile the cost of the subway fare is deducted from the card. Once the money stored on it is used up, it can be "recharged."

The Mondex system (below), is soon to be launched by a British bank. It comes with its own wallet, which contains a reader so that people can transfer money between each other's cards instead of using cash.

Smart cards have other functions – they can be used as identification devices for securing buildings or computer networks. The smart card tells the computer which parts of the network or building the user can access.

A smart card requires a simple reader so that the user can see at once how much money is left on it. Mondex provides an electronic keytab (above) for this purpose. Smart cards will be less vulnerable to theft than credit cards because if they are stolen, only the money left on the card is at risk.

Smart card networks will enable users to pay bills over the phone by feeding their smart card into a reader. The user could check the amount left on the card and be reassured that the right amount had been paid.

The idea behind British Telecom's interactive network (below) is to save time and money in producing artwork. The system allows one artist to work at a time while the others watch on their own screens.

ON/OFF
LOCK/UNLOCK
SELECT
TRANSFER
CLEAR/CANCEL
BALANCE
STATEMENT
CURRENCY
ENTER/YES
SET/CANCEL CODE
CHANGE CODE
WALLET
CARD
LOCK AVAILABLE

SMART CARDS
HOW THEY WORK

Like conventional credit cards, smart cards have a magnetic strip that identifies the user. But they also contain a microchip which has the same processing power as some of the early personal computers. Information stored on the microchip can be updated. Smart cards could have many uses. For example, they could be used to store people's medical records.

Microchip

Magnetic strip

VIRTUAL REALITY
COMPUTER ILLUSIONS

Computers have been used to create three-dimensional images for many years. "Virtual reality" allows us to take a walk inside those models, to make us feel that we are really there. Virtual reality technology uses computers to work directly on our senses – particularly vision, hearing, and touch – to create the illusion of reality, being in a computer-created spaceship or at Cluny Abbey. The user wears a special headset fitted with goggles. Computer-created images are sent to the headset. As the user moves, sensors feed data back to the computer, so that the view of the image changes, just as it would if you were moving through a real building or landscape.

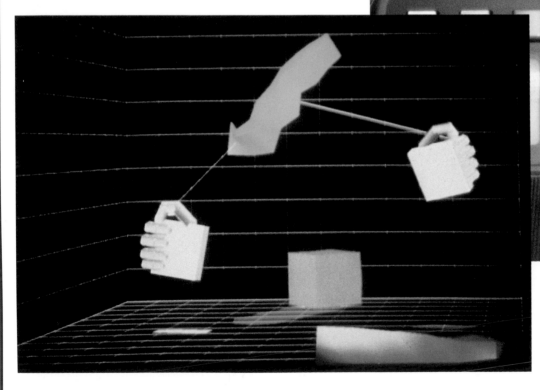

In some virtual reality systems, it is possible to pick up imaginary objects, using a glove fitted with sensors that give the impression of gripping and lifting.

Virtual reality environments like the one above have many uses. Engineers have used virtual reality to plan telephone networks.

Architects have been using three-dimensional computer-aided design programs for several years. But a virtual reality design program like the one used to create Cluny Abbey would enable them to walk inside their buildings before they are constructed.

Virtual reality can be used for entertainment or for serious scientific research. Scientists at the University of North Carolina use it to build up molecules of drugs. Virtual reality not only allows them to see how atoms bind together but to feel when they don't.

The 1000SD is the first virtual reality computer game. Put on the headset and you find yourself in a computer-generated world. The design of the headset allows you complete freedom of movement. All your actions are controlled by a joystick.

The nave of Cluny Abbey, France (below), has been rebuilt inside a computer as an exercise in virtual reality. From the archaeological discoveries, and drawings made before it was knocked down, experts created the model with the help of IBM France.

CLUNY MONASTERY
RECONSTRUCTING THE PAST

Virtual reality is a powerful tool for archaeologists. It is now possible to re-create from plans and sketches what it felt like to walk through buildings long since lost. The monastery at Cluny, in southeast France, was a great center of culture and learning during the 11th and 12th centuries. What is known of Cluny comes from excavations during the 1900s. Virtual reality still has some way to go before it is truly convincing. The graphics alone present some big problems. The headset has to respond to your movement and to send images to your eyes at least as fast as a movie.

CHRONOLOGY

WRITING & PRINTING

3500 BC The first form of writing was developed by the Sumerians.

AD 105 Paper was invented by the Chinese, replacing parchment.

1440s In Germany, Johannes Gutenberg and Johannes Fust (above) developed movable type that could be fitted together to print books.

1884 The Linotype machine was invented by a German watchmaker living in the United States – Otto Mergenthaler. It greatly increased the speed of typesetting.

1937 The first photocopier was invented by an American Chester Carlson.

1960 The Xerox Corporation developed xerography, a copying process.

TELEPHONES

1837 The first practical electric telegraph was demonstrated in the UK by William Cook and Charles Wheatstone, and installed the following year along the Great Western Railway.

1876 "Mr Watson come here, I want you" – the first telephone message – was sent by Alexander Graham Bell to his assistant. The same year Bell patented the telephone.

1891 American Almon Strowger invented an automatic exchange switching system.

1891 London was linked to the Continent by the first telephone cable under the English Channel.

1927 Transatlantic telephone services began. They depended on radio links and so were often of poor quality.

1956 The development of repeaters – boosters that could increase the power of the signal, which tended to fall away along long cables – made the first transatlantic cables possible.

1970 International Direct Dialing began operating between New York and London.

A telephone exchange, 1909

TELEVISION & RADIO

1887 Heinrich Hertz showed that waves produced by an electric spark can be detected more than 60 feet away.

1901 Italian Guglielmo Marconi sent the first messages across the Atlantic by wireless telegraphy.

1907 Lee De Forest invented the triode which enabled the amplification of radio signals.

1926 John Logie Baird invented a TV system that used infrared rays.

1929 Vladimir Zworykin developed the first electronic TV system in the United States.

1939 NBC began a regular TV service.

1947 The transistor was developed in the United States.

1951 Color TV began in the United States.

1952 The first transistor radios were marketed.

1956 Videotape was first used to record TV programs.

1975 The first home VCRs were sold.

An early color TV

COMPUTERS

1830s Charles Babbage developed his Difference Engine, a device for the mechanical compilation of mathematical tables.
1888 The results of the US Census are tabulated by a punch card system developed by Herman Hollerith, demonstrating the power of machinery to process data.
1941 German, Konrad Zuse built a program-controlled calculator using electromagnetic relays.
1946 The Electronic Numerical Integrator, And Calculator – ENIAC – was built at the University of Pennsylvania. Weighing 30 tons, with 18,000 valves, ENIAC could do 5,000 additions per second.
1958 The first all-transistor computer was made by Control Data Corporation.
1964 IBM's 360 series of computers were launched.
1975 The first personal computer, the Altair, was launched.
1977 Apple II, launched the micro-computer revolution.

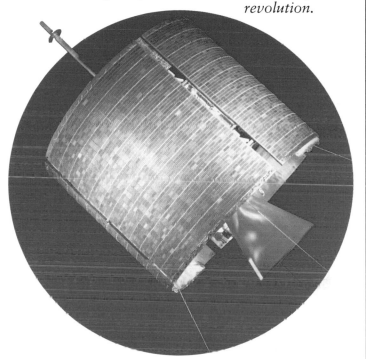

SATELLITES

1945 Arthur C. Clarke pointed out that a satellite 23,000 miles above earth would appear stationary and could be used as a relay station for worldwide communication.
1957 Sputnik, the first earth satellite was launched by the USSR.
1960 Echo 1, a large balloon 100 ft in diameter, was put into an orbit 1,100 mi. above the earth, by the United States. It was used to reflect radio signals.
1962 Telstar 1, the first successful communications satellite was launched. Telstar 1 could pick up broadcasts and retransmit them. It was the first to send live TV pictures across the Atlantic.
1965 Early Bird, the first commercial geostationary satellite, went into service, providing 240 telephone lines and one TV channel between the United States and Europe.
1980 The first of the Intelsat-V series of satellites was launched, capable of handling 12,000 telephone calls and two TV channels.
1983 The first European comsat, ECS 1, was launched by the Ariane rocket.
1986 The first DBS – direct broadcasting satellite – went into operation. By sending signals direct to dishes on individual houses, DBS bypassed the need for ground stations.

FILM & SOUND

1826 In France, Joseph Nicéphore Niepce produced the first successful photographs.
1877 Thomas Edison invented the phonograph – a way of recording sound, using a cylinder made of tin, later replaced by wax.
1895 The Lumière brothers, in France, showed moving pictures. Their key invention was the perforations at the edge of the film which move it along accurately and at the right speed.
1898 Danish inventor Valdemar Poulsen made a recording by magnetizing a steel wire.
1927 The Jazz Singer, the first "talkie" – a movie with a sound track, was made.
1933 The first stereo

GLASS-FIBER

1870 British scientist John Tyndall showed that light will follow the curved path of falling water. Light is trapped in the water and bounced from each side of the water flow.

1955 In London, Dr Narinder Kapany showed that tiny strands of glass could guide light in the same way.

1966 Two scientists from Standard Telephone Laboratories in the UK worked out that a beam of light carried through a glass fiber could carry much more information than an electrical current in a wire.

1970 Corning Glass Works produced the first glass fibers suitable for long-range communication.

1977 The General Telephone Company of California opened the world's first glass-fiber telephone link.

1988 A glass-fiber cable was laid among the US, Britain, and France, able to carry telephone, television, and data.

1989 The first glass-fiber cable was laid across the Pacific Ocean.

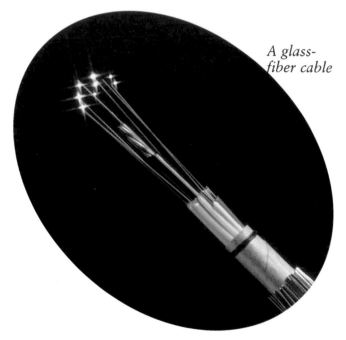

A glass-fiber cable

recordings were made by EMI in Britain.

1947 The long-playing record, revolving at 33 revolutions per minute, was developed by CBS in the United States.

1967 Ray Dolby developed a noise reduction system that improved the fidelity of recorded sound on tape.

1979 The compact disk (above) was developed by Philips and Sony.

1981 Sony marketed the first video camera, which recorded images magnetically on a disk.

1987 Digital audio tape, DAT, was developed. It combined the quality of CDs with the recordability of tape.

1988 Compact disks that could store both video, images and sound were developed.

1991 The CD-I disk became available.

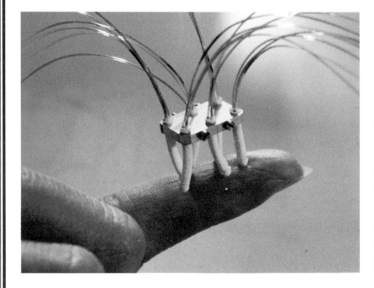

ROBOTICS

1920 The term robot was introduced by the Czech playwright Karel Capek. It is derived from the Czech word "robota" meaning drudgery.

1954 American George Devol patented a device for handling items in a factory.

1958 Engineer Joe Engleberger joined up with Devol to produce the first industrial robot.

1980 Engleberger's company, Unimation, introduced a robot called PUMA that was sensitive enough to carry out assembly tasks such as tightening nuts.

1981 Robots were introduced to car plants to weld car bodies together.

1991 A robot shearer developed by Merino Wool Harvesting in Australia can shear a sheep in half the time a human takes.

GLOSSARY

Data highway
A cable, made of glass fiber, powerful enough to carry voice, data, and even video pictures into people's homes and offices.

Digital
System in which information is stored or carried as discrete units called bits.

Etch
Means to cut away the surface of metal by using chemicals, usually an acid.

Facsimile
Literally, a copy; facsimile, (or fax) machines send copies of documents over telephone cables.

Frequency
The number of times a vibration repeats itself in a specified time – usually one second.

Geostationary
In orbit above a fixed point on the earth's surface. The higher the orbit the longer a satellite takes to complete it. At 23,000 mi, the orbit takes 24 hours, the same as the earth takes to rotate once, so the satellite remains above the same point on the earth's surface.

Interactive
System in which the user can establish a two-way exchange with a machine or computer program.

Megabyte
A computer converts all the programs and data it receives into a code – using two numbers, zero and one, called binary digits, or bits. Eight bits equals a byte and one million bytes equals a megabyte.

Molecule
The simplest form of a chemical compound that can exist, consisting of two or more atoms of different elements.

Network
Computers linked together so that they can exchange data. A network can be local (in an office, for example), national, or international.

Photogravure
High-quality printing process using plates on to which the picture is etched in the form of cells – shallow cells, which hold little ink, for light colors, and deeper cells for darker colors.

Program
Set of instructions for a computer. Also called software.

Semiconductor
A substance, such as silicon, whose conductivity can be controlled by small amounts of impurities.

Refractive index
The degree to which a substance such as glass or water bends light entering it.

Videophone
Telephone that enables you to see as well as hear the person to whom you are connected.

INDEX